Places We Were Never Meant to See

Meant to See

Places We Were Never
Meant to See

Brian Thornton

INK
BRUSH
PRESS

ISBN: 978-0-9909452-2-2
Library of Congress Control Number: 2015945371

Manufactured in the United States

Ink Brush Press
Austin, Texas

This book is dedicated to
a boy buried in Baghdad

Poetry from Ink Brush Press

Acknowledgments

I am grateful to the editors of the these journals for publishing some of the poetry now in this book:

Amarillo Bay
Breakwater Review
IKP (International Kurdish Press)
On Human Flourishing: An Anthology of Eudemonic Poetry
War, Literature, and The Arts

Special thanks to James Merrill, TS Eliot, Adrienne Riche, Elizabeth Bishop, and Robert Lowell for helping with the tent riggings.

CONTENTS

Section One:
Shots in Soft Focus

On Blindness

To be blind means to listen
as others feast on vision,
to mouth dry bread, unaware
the lion's share
is laid across the table—
his head filled with honey,
the sweet comb sunk
into empty sockets,
a parody, perhaps,
of those who taste
and see and take
refuge in a mirror now
obscured by greased
fingers groping for the salt.

Macular Degeneration

A painting ruined by rain,
memory maintained
for a few moments
then fading as days
erase even the darkest shades
left on a drying sidewalk.

Arabic Love Song

Habibi, whose eyes I'll never see,
the past has stolen you from me.
My sight replaced with memories—
the memories of your eyes, habibi.

Habibi, are you still with me
or have you found someone who sees?
Replaced my sight with memories—
the memories of my eyes, habibi.

Habibi, will you help me see?
Take apart the world for me,
replace all of the memories—
the memories through your eyes, habibi.

Habibi, will you still love me
even though I cannot see,
or will you replace my memory
with memories of other eyes, habibi?

Doughnut Holes

I.

I had a thing for donuts as a child—
Dad and I would walk to Mister Sweet's
every morning. My eyes would still be filled
with sleep, hair tousled, shuffling feet
heavy with the weight of early mornings.
Gravity, though, ended at the crosswalk
as signatures of sugar started pouring
vigor into each new step I took.
Dad would buy me long-johns for a nickel
and he would get a chocolate topped with nuts.
He'd furl his face and give my rib a tickle—
"A donut with no hole? That's not a donut."

I bit into my treat and shrugged my shoulders.
Who knew the holes would come as I grew older?

II.

Who knew? As I grew older, the holes
and vacancies began to take their toll.
Halfway seeing, but fully feeling the fact.
I must learn to live with blindness. It's an act
of passive study— you learn to closely listen
for the hiss of cars and steps of children,
beeps at the ends of books; you learn to hear
the soft synthetic speech of crosswalks cleared;
to sit on sidelines, silently scribbling gestures
in your head because you can't quite picture
the paper or the ball; and you learn to be
told, in replay, what you didn't see.
They cheer as injured players leave the game
but I sit silent, jealous of their pain.

III.

With silent jealousy, I sat in pain—
scalded, simply pouring morning coffee.
I considered a companion to help me
around the house. I heard that she had trained
for years, but wouldn't mop or sweep.
She wouldn't wash my mirrors or my windows,
or fix the door, or help me hang my clothes,
but they insisted she'd be very cheap.
Still, I couldn't justify the cost.
The problem was, she wouldn't read to me,
which I said was a necessity;
and so, regrettably, the sale was lost.
My blindness may be trying, I concede,
but a dog is something I refuse to *need*.

IV.

Thank you, but I just don't need a dog.
I'd rather be the stumbling, groping fool
than a ghost behind a drooling pool
of "ooh's" and "ah's" and their constant bog
of oglers wanting to know the mongrel's name.

The Doc: *The dog could be a conversation
starter, or a spark of admiration...*

Sure—for the dog! I shouldn't blame
someone still possessing faculties.
You see, they'll smile and nod at his devotion
but who will want to bother with the notion
that I can gauge the weather by the breeze?

The doctor rubbed his glasses with a tissue.
I don't believe your eyes are quite the issue.

V.

They say my issue isn't with my eyes
but rather with the way I choose to see.
I manifest my ghosts, and visualize
a future fading darker as it flees.
The memory of green is now a distant
whisper of December pines and paper
torn at Christmas time, but then persistent
silence wipes my children from my future.

I feel no love left for me—from God,
from girl, from family. The hot
iron in my sockets marks Your absence,
rejected from the Kingdom in Your silence.
Just kiss the little lambs that You like best,
and pull Your purple curtain east to west.

VI.

From east to west, the purple curtain closed,
drawn by dampened attar of a rose
beneath my window. Like a quiet burglar
barely heard above approaching thunder,
the bush brushed, staccato, on the sill—
relentless tapping, wearing down my will,
curled beneath a blanket on the floor
until I couldn't take it anymore.

Scent and sound teases me with sight.
Blackbird, take my nose. Painter, show
your strokes to hands now bleeding, clenched tight
and cut across the knuckles from the window.

I held my bleeding eyes in shattered panes
and saw the world inside a drop of rain.

VII.

I saw the world inside a drop of rain—
a tear, dropped beneath the disco ball,
painted the first shine I'd seen since walls
stole the stars. I thought of window panes
as she asked a boy to dance and laughter roared
because, he said, she couldn't hear the song.
I took her hand, prepared to prove him wrong.
The blind man led the deaf girl to the floor.

I tapped a solid rhythm on her waist
as she guided me through donut holes. She smelled
like father-memories in a cloudless sky.
I kissed her neck, and I began to taste
stories I needed desperately to tell:
I had a thing for donuts as a child...

Paradox of Peripheral Vision

"The peripheral retina is very sensitive to dim objects and relative motion. When the central retina is damaged, the patient may not be able to see faces straight ahead but may see stars in the sky or a speck of paper on the floor."

—awareness brochure distributed by the Macular Degeneration
Foundation

I'm not really sure about your eyes,
but your ears look lovely in this light.
Your smile, I'm told, could make a blind man see.
Sorry. But the bit of tikka in your teeth
shows you have sophisticated taste.
Please forgive my staring at your waist,
but the periphery mountains are amazing—
little lint sheep in meadows grazing
on steep cliffs; some resting in the shade
of a Mirabelle tree in late
September across your shoulder, now asleep.
How I want so bad to be a sheep
instead of me pretending to see the ewe—
the you those ewes are holding tightly to.

Un Chien Andalou

The padded vise holds my head
snug like a nun's habit draped sterile
in fear of what the doctor gods must do
with those knives and needles resting
on the table and I have to wonder
if Himler was an ophthalmologist
if he too wondered what hid behind
the ocular cavities of his patients
in Dachau or Auschwitz God damn
the fear I can't think straight my eyes
fixed on the neat and precise duplicity
laid out on that metal tray just above
my chin one set for each eye as to not
cross contaminate the cuts and Christ
the searing pain like a cigarette stabbed
into my temple promises I will feel no further
but remember always the disjoined effect
of one eye in place as the other slowly
scans the room controlled by curved forceps
as if half of my body has simply stood up
to meet the stare of the surgeon I want
to throw up I want to close my eyes
just to close my eyes and allow
the cadent strobes to flicker
like the shadow of the death moth
growing fainter and fainter until the ether
brings a simplicity of still horses
the comfort of a closed carousel

Understanding Zombies

1.   You do not grope with your chin,
and your hand is not desperate to touch.
It is simply hoping for an empty
path.

2.   Your eyes don't prefer to be
closed. They read the sound
of blackness, open—

3.   Your first steps will be shy. They will ask
for details— implications
in the sandpaper of concrete,
the garbled speech
of gravel.

4.   There is risk
in picking your feet up off the ground.
Your foot will know
negative space by its silence.

5.   Your mind may find shadows
of memories misplaced
inches away from where your keys
should be.

6.   Your body
must cry the humiliation
of being led through
labyrinths by the force
of friends, or others paid
to stagger
at your pace. They will try
to be your sight,
narrating beyond
the frame and learning

how to tell
stories.

7.   Your eyes must cry, believing
in the disappointment
of what you can no longer see.

Scooter

I.

I used to know the freedom of two wheels
wearing warm grooves in kettle-shined
aging roads. I used to know the real
power of high numbers— four hundred fine
stallions locked in tight quarters shaking
the Earth beneath impatient stamping hooves.
And the release, oh the release, quaking
asphalt fading into smooth removes;
Serpentine, nine-to-five behind,
and two hundred miles from where the day
meets the dust, leaning into the wind
as moon beams bend lingering shadows astray...
Freedom, elusive bastard of the blind.
Recollections, road rash of the mind.

II.

The bright colors of memory seem to pale
against this drying portrait on my flesh:
Smooth salmon strokes dotted with brailed
amber pockets of pus, textures fresh
from scrubbing with a steel sterile brush—
a morphine Matisse. I am Avant Garde.
I am fragments shored against my rush
into loose gravel. I am a chord
exposed. Dissonant jazz-tangled tendons
dance with dirt, persistent, beneath my skin—
Charleston, Charleston, flapping flesh falls scarred,
Devil dances in the Big Band bone yard
making me remember tender bends in
freshly paved roads once again.

III.

Heart balances broken vision, but pride
Alone leaves a widening fissure to fester.
Rain falls harder, faster, like a jester
Lost to lions after laughter died.
Everything is broken. Broken bike
Yawns beneath broken awning. Broken
Door bangs broken arm. Scream as broken
Aerosmith record skips— Dude looks like...
Velvet...velvet...velvet after the rain.
No light. Bulb's broke. Wife broke for Maine
Days ago. (She had a thing for eyes.).
Strafing winds send painful chills as I
Open the dented door and walk back in,
Never to leave this broken home again.

IV.

The open road has quite a future in sales—
Waiting like the mantis for weakened meat,
then springing like the leopard on its frail
victim. I was easy prey for sweet
talk. My friend came by on a winding whine
of tiny promise and told me to take a ride.
I paced around the small device, a wine
red and cool cream scooter, as pride
snickered, amused by this reduced flicker
of freedom. I straddled the low leather seat
with a shrug and bore down on the kicker
then rolled away with hesitant dragging feet.
One hundred yards was all it took to find
the art of Zen and maintenance to the mind.

V.

I thought I would regret the slower pace—
losing the lean of man and machine pitched
just inches above the blurring blacktop's face;
or the momentary, broomed-witch,
weightless lift of down-shifting kicks
that shorten the straight tired stretches of long
highway into seconds with a flick
of the wrist. I was so wrong.
I missed so much riding to fulfill
a man-measured machismo, like the reason
the roads tend to bend through the hills—
Golden grasses beneath the slow sway
of willow boughs burdened with bickering Jays.
Such splendid scenery of seasons
redefines my selfish take on freedom.

A Trying Ghost

I wonder if the little girl
who used to haunt our hallway
when I was ten
has found someone more faithful,
or if, by chance, she still stands
in front of the closet door,
assigned to a blind man
who wishes she was still there.

A Sense of Seasons

1. Autumn

Because I have
been told,
I know the leaves
are turning.

Wind no longer
carries calm
streams, but the rasp
of rattlesnakes.

My foot—a stiff
jaw closing
on potato chips.
The shit-smell of death

composting in the bed
of fresh-cut
flower stems
next door
reminds me
I once knew
gold:
broken

and scattered like
a puzzle
beneath my feet.

2. Winter

The closest you'll ever be to seeing what I see—
the sunglassed-snowman
obscured by frosted
windows, naked
trees eased into
invisibility, your hands
blocking eyes from stiff
winds. The sterile
landscape of Sunday morning
before the smoke
and soot of the truly devout leaves
specks and streaks
on broken roads,
the droves of snow
that close those roads
and blow bouts
of blindness over
entire cities;
the careful steps, avoiding
children's throws;
the pity for those without
electricity, left in the dark;
and the long sigh
as you think about
the park where you sat last
Summer and complained
about the heat.

3. Spring

In the cemetery
the groundskeeper is cutting
the grass for the first time.
The moan of the mower
bothers neither the dead
nor the sparrows singing
elegies beneath the leaves.

Potted flowers left
for fathers— memory
mixing with the trailing mulch.
Fresh cut grass slips
between my sandal straps
as I sit and trace
the raised letters
on my grandmother's stone.

The dash between
her years shortened
by sickness,
but long enough to keep me
coming another year
to talk about the weather
while the mower
drones in the background.

4. Summer

Roses and jasmine freshly planted
 in the courtyard, and someone is stoking
their grill with Ronsonol. The painter's
cigarette competes with dryer sheets
churning in the laundry mat across the street.

Its late enough in the day to hear the crickets—
little fiddlers hidden beneath the occasional
rustle of dried leaves. The doves purr in deep eaves;
grackles gripe in the grass and scatter
from the barking charge of a small dog.

There is a flavor to the first days of Summer—
the wet salt on one's lips, the stippled attar
of the chlorine in the public pool that hangs
on the tip of the tongue with each breath;
the delicate foam of a fresh drawn beer.

Let me sit here in my midnight, the stone
bench sweating on my back, shed buds
of a hyacinth tickling my shoulder, falling
between my fingers and surely in my hair.
Then let the evening bring the chance for you to see.

Section Two:
Behind The Big Red Tent

Tumbleweeds

A tumbleweed is really Russian Thistle
but in its death it finds itself
redefined by movement,
unearthed
and free
from Spring's stillness,
while we stay stuck, waiting
for wind to tell us who we are.

A Carnival in New Mexico, 1986

For as I walked around and looked carefully at your objects of
worship, I even found an altar with this inscription: TO AN
UNKNOWN GOD. So you are ignorant of the very thing you
worship—and this is what I am going to proclaim to you.
                                                    —Acts 17:23

Walking across the midway,
I saw a tent that travelled
all the way from Russia with a promise
of things we'd never seen before.

As I looked carefully at the objects
of childish wonder, the altars
inscribed to unknown beasts,
I felt the soft touch of ignorance.

Most were dead—
the Chupacabra, the jackalope,
the bare-breasted mermaid rigid
under scratched glass.
What made it work was the living—
the two-headed calf that cowered
in the corner, the shaved wallaby
(said to be the world's largest rat.)

More than twenty years now, I am standing
inside this tent again. How well the stitches
are hidden on the alligator boy from Borneo.
I can barely see the duct tape on his tail.

The feathers of the thunderbird have thickened,
and Ropen's claws now rest
beside a cast of Caddy's shed,

but one pedestal is bare—

an open proclamation of curiosity.

A calliope calls the curtain
as the thylacine falls asleep
inside her kennel, and the last-known
unicorn stamps his hoof.

Tent Rigging #1: A Laying of Hands

Just off the midway, by the pizza and Coca-Cola,
spotlights bounce harshly off the snake woman's sign.
And the eyes of two—the barker and the beauty—
darken, one with kindness, one to see inside our open wallets.
They have come gladly from their trailers
to welcome my friend and me.
We step through the turnstile into the dim tent
where (I like to think) she has been waiting all day, alone.
She smiles tensely, unable to hide her relief
that someone actually came.
Her head in the box bows with practiced timidity. She hates
herself.
There is no loneliness like hers.
In character once more,
she flicks a slit tongue and asks our names in hisses.
I would like to hold her slender body in my arms,
to know why she has chosen these false scales
sunk around her jaws.
She is green and yellow.
Her hair falls disconsolate on her forehead,
a light breeze making it itch. I move it away,
delicately reaching beyond the guardrail on tip toes.
She smiles and I realize
that if I reached back and unlatched the clasps around the box, I
would break
into myth.

Marcus The Wolf Man Offers Me a Job

All I had to do was swing the hammer,
ring the bell to win a *Krokus* mirror—
the last I needed for my wall of rock
legends, bare between *Ratt* and *Dokken*.
The lying smiles of starving carny workers,
taught by Marcus, a smallish werewolf barker,
his perfect— surgically sharp and white,
tiny knives honed to practiced sleight.
I might as well have worn a red bandana,
and told him I was on my way to Grandma's
house. I knew I should have walked away
a mirror better for it. Instead, I stayed
for seven weeks in search of poets' mirrors
at $5.15 an hour swinging hammers.

Tent Rigging #2: Texas Exodus

The trucks pushed through it.
Just the worst time of the year
for a carnival, and what a trip!
Dirt cut crisp into tent riggings.
The tarps tore, weathered to rash
on the invisible Kansas highway,
and the camels from the petting zoo,
nostrils vexed and caked
with snot and sand, lying down
in the bare-barred trailer. I wondered
if they could remember summer:
being led to shallow slopes
on the Brazos while a fat man
shoveled their shit and matted their beds,
ran from trailer to trailer hoping
there will be time and money enough
for Georgia Moon and a gas station whore.

The dirt was so bad
we duct-taped vents and windows,
and papered the worn weather-stripping.
The Wichita wind, what a bitch!
The parade pushed on all night,
sleeping in snatches,
voices on an AM radio pushed
in and out of white noise—
Aliens...already here...we are...
technology...after the break...
Around dawn, we came down
to a temperate valley outside of Garden City,
with concrete slabs and windmills
beating the darkness, three pump jacks
on the flat horizon, and a stray white cow
chewing the cud in a meadow.

We pulled into a roadside park.
There were old nests above the bathroom door
and a shit cost a quarter. We were happy
just to stand up
until Marcus said we missed a turn
almost ninety miles back.
We got back on the bus and found
the fairgrounds by noon;
they were (you might say) alright.
All this after being here
just a week, and I would do it again,
but get this: I traveled
all that way not just for a paycheck
but to escape the monotony of selling
vacuum cleaners from door to door—the rejection
of tired excuses and screen-door barricades.
There was a paycheck, certainly,
but that wasn't the point.
I had escaped before, but thought
this time would be different;
this escape, crawling out of my skin,
was hard and bitter agony, like our paychecks.
And nothing happened! Leaving children
with inflatable aliens and cheap dolls,
we returned to our busses, ready
for the real escape. We will see
what happens once we cross the Kansas border.

Science of the Snake Lady

To what I will become—
You who sit beside me.
Legs, now visible, and draped
across faded velour bus seats,
the suit of who you are
wadded on the floor
like a loose nucleus.
The truth of who you were
hanging in the ether
like particles of dust
aggravated by your own voice.
The particles of those particles—
the gluons and spinons
of stories you tell
of the iron-shaped scar
on your cheek, the quarks
of hiding in the closet,
running away and meeting Marcus,
the alleles that link you to past and present
like the trailer hitches
on the camel cages
pulling one more connection
closer to the surface.
Our pasts, our chemistry,
bonded in who we must become,
repelled by the reasons,
holds us in stasis
on a bus just outside
of Dalhart, Texas.
This is all a trick of the eye,
the two of us sitting here,
the dust outside, the driver
finishing his cigarette.
The reality lies
in the next town where we both
will climb into our boxes,

tell children stories
we have well rehearsed,
 and smile.

But now, as the sun sets,
all we do is crawl back into our illusion and wait.

Tent Rigging #3: In the Changing Room

In Tulsa, Oklahoma,
I went with our gorilla
to her first performance
and sat and waited for her
in the backstage changing room.
The tent was crowded. It was dark
inside—a bustling room
full of eager people.
The gorilla was inside
what seemed like a long time
and while I waited I read
an old *National Enquirer*
used to line the cages
of the snakes and lizards.
I studied the photographs:
Mary in a water stain,
crude, and full of mildew.
Clinton and the Alien,
a dead man propped on a pole—
Lazarus, the caption read.
Babies with alligator heads,
mouths tied with string.
I turned the page and saw
a familiar face, wound in
scales too shiny to be real.

Suddenly, from inside
the small crowded tent
came the gorilla's cues—
the whimper of a woman
morphing to the masculine
gruff snorts and roars
as the cage breaks.
I didn't even flinch,
accustomed to the act—
simply a beautiful woman

spun on a steel platform
under cover of strobe lights.
It was kind of embarrassing
how many people bought it
and ran from the tent in terror.
The problem was, it wasn't
just the gorilla's voice,
or just the gorilla's hands
gripping steel bars.
It was my hands clenched
around outdated pages,
around a realization—
some primal understanding
forcing us into chorus.
I was a gorilla.
I—we—were banging, banging
the heavy bars on the cage,
our eyes fixed on the picture
in the *National Enquirer*.
In just twelve hours, I was
meant to marry Ilsa—
a new angle, my head
locked in mirrored boxes,
babysitting hatchlings;
children standing around
a rope, teasing us
with trash and tired insults.
But, then again, why not?
Why couldn't I lose my legs
and crawl into that cramped
cavity for a few hours?
I peeked through the frayed
opening near the bottom
of her tent. I saw
her swollen knees, torn
sun dress, and shoeless calluses,
the freak behind the freak—
a headless rape victim

surrounded by feet, children's
feet, reflected infinitely
in polished spirit mirrors.
I never felt so strange.
How could I be a snake?
A gorilla? A Brian?
Sure, I was in love
with the voice lodged
in my throat, even
with the *National Enquirer*
and those shellacked scales.
But that didn't change
the fact I had to stifle
a scream hidden behind
faded yellow canvas.
The strobe lights stopped,
but my eyes still flashed
with big black spots
another, and another.

Then I was back in the changing room.
The show was over. Outside,
in Tulsa, Oklahoma,
were rides, and games, and shows,
and it was still the twelfth
of August, 1998.

Remember the Jackalope

I saw you once beneath a gnarled
salt cedar sapling. Then you moved,
ruining the illusion.
But for that moment,
in our fixed stances, you with budded laurels,
me in a sun-bleached baseball cap,
old water began to flow,
and your brief repose
reminded me of creatures
stolen from the shadows
by logic and newer masters—
trading cards and toy dinosaurs:
an entire phylum buried
for ten years in tar
preserved but forgotten just below
the surface of belief.

Tent Rigging #4: Climbing Into the Box

First, having read the book of myths,
and painted my face,
and checked my fangs were straight,
I put on
the snake skin turtleneck
and the absurd turban.
I am having to do this
not like Lazarus Colloredo with his
parasitic brother, Baptista,
attached to his sternum,
but here alone.

There is a box.
The box is always there
in the middle of the big red tent.
We know what it is for,
we who have used it.

I climb in,
latching the clasps.
My new coiled body immerses me.
The pale lights
reflect in the spirit glass,
mirrors under the table top
hiding the human illusion.
I sit down.
The concrete cripples me,
and I squirm like a pinned hen before her neck snaps
and there is no one
to tell me when the show
will begin.

The tent blushes from
the sun bleeding through red canvas
of the Win-a-Fish penny toss,
and my fangs are powerful.

They pump the venom with childish nightmares,
but the stage is another story:
I have to learn alone
to keep my body still or the box will
squeeze my neck
and force unconscious black.

And now: It is easy to forget
what I came for
among the Tocci Twins and Pin Heads
still living here
in fixed repose beneath box fans.
Besides,
you breathe differently here, or not at all.

I came to explore the living dead.
Their words are purposes.
Their words are maps.
I came to see the brief belief in small gospels
and the damage undone by doubt—
the seed of what we know choked
by the weeds of what we wanted
to believe.

The thing I came for:
the trick itself and not the secret of the trick,
the levitation rather than the levers,
the fixed face of the mermaid
hanging above the Tent of Wonders entrance,
the evidence of conjecture
worn down to its purest by a man in a clever box,
his mechanically undulating skin
coiled in its assertion
among tentative children.

This is the place,
and I am here, *homis reptilia*, scales and hair
stained black, the sideshow in armored plexiglass.

The children circle silently
around the room
and dive into hypothesis.
I am them. I am

the extra leg of Frank Lentini, the skin
between the Karas twins,
the silver and copper traded for tickets,
paid to a pygmy on a rotting
empty barrel.
We are the half-debunked claims
that once bound entire tribes,
the god's dog,
the fouled phoenix.
We are, I am, you are,
by axiom or folly,
the one who still buys
a rocking horse moment
with Irish gold
and smiles at the circus flyer
checking your watch
to see what time we appear.

Snake Boy To The Chupacabra

You and I are nothing
more than attractions
fixed in tried tradition.
My legs, entwined,
hidden behind mirrors marred
with popcorn grease
and disbelief; yours,
styrofoam behind twisted
wires, brittle and taped
in desperate defiance
of time, knowing
that real was never
real—an ocelot with sewn
shark's teeth, a man
in a magic box.
We are no longer
legend. We are reduced
to Russian thistle rooted
by the hooked end of a question,
paralyzed by the parentheticals
on our tarnished plaques.

We should go then, somewhere you
have never been.
Never mind the mesquites;
their tender brambles
our only tethers
in a tumbleweed parade
across another quiet highway.

Tent Rigging #5: Home After Ten Years Away

Gone now, the pygmy on the pedestal,
a lion's voice who drew a queue
along the Tent of Wonders,
the Burmese python around his neck
hanging sedate like a scaled shawl.
There is just a man in a blue shirt,
bored and sweating, smoking a cigarette
in front of a fading marquee.

My daughter holds her ground, afraid to go in.
I hold up her chin,
we both grin, and I brush her hair behind her ears.
I tell her we are safe.
She dabs her cheeks
afraid to meet what I once was. Though,
she too has thoughts of changing her skin—
a princess, an airplane, a mannequin.
I tell her I was once the human snake.
She believes me, and takes
my hand, resolute,
a big girl with drying tears.
Now, I return.

Her grip on my leg, gone:
Her fingers now press
on the glass of a princess—
a mannequin in a mermaid tail.
She doesn't ask me if it is real
but rather where it came from.
I ignore the small piece of duct tape
under the poorly-placed hair piece
and tell her about the *Tyrolian Islands*
off the coast of *Sebasia*, as we make
our way through the slow moving queue,
and I hear a familiar hiss whispering
from the alcove ahead. It is her turn

to talk to the snake, to ask questions
collected like Russian artifacts or tissue
on a tumbleweed. We walk in
together, bramble-bodies at the mercy of the wind.

Epilogue: Showman's Rest Cemetery

"Weighing 607 pounds, Bruce Snowdon was a sideshow fat man from 1977 to 2003, billed as "Harold Huge." His death on November 9th, 2009, at the age of 63 marks the end of a long, heavy tradition dating back centuries."
                                        —Miami Herald, *January 19, 2010*

1.

The last great fat man lies beneath
the dull halo dancing from Crab Girl's lantern—
a small light for small people gathered
to keep the wick of self-respect from dying.

The light is blinding to the crying albino
who went from tent to tent on chilly evenings
carrying a flashlight and food for all the freaks—
Diogenes in search of fried chicken,
an honest meal for a man in the back of a truck,
axles bent and bowing beneath the weight
of satisfaction, the simple curve of laughter
cut into his broad jiggling jowls,
three degrees beneath a twelve foot belt—
Quantum theory traded for kids with crayons.

2.

In the cemetery, still clowns repose
on curved stones, and God-given names,
smaller than the monikers enclosed
in quotes footnote their now-quiet fame,
the dash between the dates extended past
fifteen minutes in a big red tent
filled with children, stocked with cynics who laughed
with you, not just at you, in the end.

The carnival code lives in the coins on your eyes.
You were carried by a crane from your room
into another adorned with angels, (disguised
sideshows), chubby cherubs compared to you.
Chiseled in the granite above your stone,
the last known unicorn stamps his hoof.

Section Three:
Excavations

Christmas In Trafalgar Square
London, England

The lamps light the iron lions ready
to leap to life at the untimely
stroke of an old clock.
They seem to stand sentry
over the protesters'
posters of dead babies
and skinned foxes
along the busy boulevard.
 A drone drawn
from the base
of a lonely pine—
a choir holding plastic candles
swaying and shivering
as shoppers go on shopping
without breaking stride.

By the glass elevator leading down
to small shops and pay-toilets,
a small manger with wooden angels
blocks the wind for a small boy
with one leg. He pushes *play*
on a cheap CD player and the metal
taps on the bottom of his single shoe
rattle like a snake's tail.
The sound of pence and pounds
falling in a filling bucket
betrays his cadence,
along with the persistent choir
in the background
who asks in ¾ time,
"What child is this?"
The Christ child flakes and fades
under tears
of melting snow,
 swaddled in a still

cradle, eyes fixed
on the backs
of the clapping crowd
as the lamb beneath the lions
takes a shaky bow.

Here is Christ Confined
Madrid, Spain

Eyes chained to a downward gaze of cold marble
in the sun-speared transept
of the Monesterio del San Jeronimo Real.

Confined to stare back, wanting, at our eyes waiting
for forgiveness, Father's promises,
or hoping to hear the *Eli, Eli, Eli* of an unfortunate son.
The continued crucifixion
of critics who comment on the coagulating blood
of God-forced brush strokes
chokes the aesthetic appeal
of ancient barbarisms captured on fading canvas.

Confined to our sense of shame,
the exquisite pain of iron stakes pushed
through skin and bone,
piercing the petrifying grains
of a sun-bleached cross
lost to other artists next door at the Prado.

In the Kitchen of a Statue

Pompeii

On the wall her shadow jumps behind my camera flash—
 Rainfall hitting stale gray ash.

Outside the Vatican on Easter Sunday
Rome, Italy

Back home, in Texas, my daughter tries
to sleep, stirred by the flicker
of street lights and her mother on the phone.
The sun is rising over Rome
as the dry gate wheezes open, and the vicar's
voice drowns my wife's goodbye.

In her morning (in my evening) she will hide
a basket full of colored eggs
under rocks and press them into Pampas grass,
but for now she helps to pass
the time as I wait in line, leaning against wine kegs,
hoping to get inside.

The wall I wait beside is cool against our backs,
the fresh white mortar veins—
a bronchial mesh hidden behind the pleas
of supermarket posters, the clean
grout encasing cells of old stones, stained
and stippled by time and tack.

Around ten, the crowd's necks crane
down the narrow road.
Its tall villas bouncing benedictions—distant
whispers indistinct
from the murmurs rising in the crowd
drowning why they came.

By noon I know I've missed it all.
The multitudes reverse
and look for busses, quiet cafes, or open bars.
The streets congest with cars,
so I sit, unmoved, until they all disperse
like lemmings to the fall.

In my evening, (in her morning) my daughter pulls
apart the Pampas grass to find
her first pink egg as my wife sits against the fence back home.
The sun is setting over Rome
as the dry gate wheezes closed behind
our shadows on the wall.

Clandestino

Sevilla, Spain

Sitting here today on this empty
patio, I remember the way
the old man sat in the corner—
hands crossed on top
of his cane, a shallow
smile like the curve
of an old canoe rising
above his aging jowls.

I remember the tap
of that cane, the ghostly
reverberations of the echo
coming back through
the empty corridors,
the malleable speed of sound
creating a chorus
of rich clicks—
the spirit of flamenco
searching for a dancer.
I remember how he tipped
his head, brief but noticeable
as you and I waved and walked
toward the next empty room,
and how he called us to him,
away from our tour group,
with the slow circle
of his hand—shaky, but somehow
steady enough for him
not to care.

I remember his voice as he spoke
only to us, asking if we believed
in miracles—*en las verdades
de los santos*. You said
yes, and I said nothing,

but the answer was enough
for him to rise to his feet,
creaking like the lid
of an old locker and how he hobbled,
both hands still on his cane,
to a doorway split by the shadow
of late afternoon, and blocked
by a single fraying rope
that our tour guide walked past
already engaged in the story
of the next open chamber.

I remember he told us
to be *cuidado*
as we stepped across
the barricade, and the first
of the miracles as he skipped nimbly
over the rope himself
like Dorothy's scarecrow
just plucked from his perch
and healed with the power
of an off-screen orchestra.

I remember the chamber—
a small dark room save for one
window, its bright beam trained
to the time of day on a small pot
placed in the corner almost cowering
like a beaten prisoner, and I remember
the small buds reaching
for the sun, not red or yellow,
but grey and ashen, still tight
like the spent folds of a good cigar.

I remember the second miracle—
the child-like tone
of the old man's voice,
the animation of his belief,

70

and the way the shadows concealed
his age, turning him into a boy
again as he told us about the room,
how the flowers only bloom
when the church bells ring
for the passing of a saint
or the death of a king,
how this same sprig has stayed
for over 100 years, and doesn't know
the difference between
winter or spring.

I remember the look
on your face, and the tickle
in the back of my brain
caused by your expression—
the nucleus of faith,
not born from his story,
but from your acceptance
of the story.

Today, I sit in the same empty patio,
and I remember you. The old man
is not in the corner. The shadow—
completely covering
the doorway with the fraying rope.
But I know what is sitting down the hall,
and I know that the soft smell
of the attar comes from that room
as I fall, like a weak mind at the end
of a pocket watch,
back into our Sevilla.

Je T'aime, Marie

Paris, France

In a corner of the catacombs,
sixteen skulls stare, fixed
to the border of a brittle heart.
Each one balanced on a small white shelf
made from ribs and wrists with delicate fingers
under a stiff jaw. The heart inside,
stippled with the tips of unmatched femurs,
stands in morbid remembrance
of the girl, Marie, named
in the dimly lit plaque leaning
below the long rows of those, nameless
here, that we now pay to see.

Photographs Taken in a Cemetery
Brussels, Belgium

The steep slits, sliced
into hard ground
with heavy shovels,
line the snow-covered cemetery
like stilled black keys
on a piano.

The shadow of two crossed sticks
reach out and meet
my shadow like two old friends
shaking hands
before my shadow pulls away,
moving from the stillness
and the pallor of flowers
beginning to wither in the chill.

The now-falling snow
seals the wounds in whiteness
and erases the newness
left by a man with a shovel;
the flowers crossed
on the lid of the casket
disappear, and the footprints
leading to where I stand—
now a smooth plane
as if I was never even here.

Standing on the Edge of the Earth
Sagres, Portugal

Today, I sit on the cliff
that, 500 years ago,
marked the end of the world.
My feet swing over
the precipice, the surf
twenty stories below,
stiff winds buffeting
my legs back and forth
like bobs on withered strings
ready to snap,
the swells strong enough
to send a spray of wet salt
high enough to sting my eyes.

This is the same cliff
where Cristobal and Vasco
peered into the stirring surf—
a blue bruised face pocked
with whirlpools,
the sinister smile of sea foam
clinging to the jagged rocks
in the low tide,

waiting for me,
as it did for them.
I wonder if they felt as small
as I do here—infinitesimal
to the point of weightless,
as if the wind could simply
pick them up and carry
them across and over
the edge of the Earth.
I wonder, if, in their microcosm
they wanted to scream,

or at least write a poem,
and if that seed is what began
the reimagining of maps,
the building of ships, the sermons
in pubs to drunk sailors.
I wonder if I, standing here
in torn jeans and tennis shoes,
could write a ship
or a pair of wings.
Should I step back slowly and go home.
or just fall forward
and see what will happen?

Spring Break With Gypsies
Andalusia, Spain

I.

He can't help wondering tonight
if it is the beer, the music, or the feet
on his pillow that keep him awake.
 All he knows is that this old town
Wakes children from tradition. Everything he has been told
 is wrong—how to ask for a drink,
how to be honest, how to feel, how to tell someone
how he feels, how to sit and think
about the beginning of the day, how to begin
the day alone, how to fall
down the stairs, how to fall
by the wayside,
how to fall,
how to fall,
how to fall
into the old cliché of walking
hand in hand through empty city streets,
how to be American,
how to
write.
Spain—this machine kills
modesty. Reduced to one child
confused— how to go home,
how to simply say
the words that they already know.

He feels he may have gone too far.
After all, they are in Spain
with adobe on the ceiling, angels
on the wall, and ebera floors that hold
the gravity of rain,
the gravity of words spoken too soon,
the gravity of tradition waiting

to be separated like the statues
of Italica from their manhood.

He tries to bridge the gap
with honesty, and in return
they rest like Pisces on a single bed,
separated by the truth
of Cruz Campo. He doesn't want it.
 He doesn't want it.
He just wants it to be said,
to let the ether between them hold
the faint scent of what will never be.

II.

Awake again and listening to midnight
in the old city—the soft voices of whores
feeding addiction, the twitching hiccup
of a lost starling, interruption from a speeding pizza.

His hand is open on the pillow. Soft breeze
drying the day's sweat from the creases
in his palms, cool cotton cradling
tired tendons, interrupted by the touch of her fingers

      interlocking with his.

She can't see him, so she squeezes
his hand and calls him by name. He looks
to her and sees open eyes reflected
in midnight—candle dance, candle dance, blink,
one candle dances down
to the pillow.
He says nothing, interrupted
by his hand being pulled—pulled
toward her, pulled toward the *yes* fire.

He feels wet
lips push against
his hand, against where holes
should be, where nails should be
driven, nails that might support the gravity
of this moment—heart beat quickened, nervous vomit
rising to his chest, interrupted
by words

      he never thought he would hear from her.

He is afraid now—
afraid of the persistence
of fire

still staring
back at him,
interrupted
by involuntary movement

He takes his hand
back, and trades
her words for drapery—curtain
arm set soft on her
shoulder, body twist
to welcome sleep
away from fish
tailed feet to the head,
sleep welcomed lies
of friendship pushed
like an untethered sloop
in fast currents.

The boat can never return.

Waves push seaward, interrupted
by words

He never thought he would say.
A whale escapes
her chest. Candles die
slowly. Two
then four. This is all
he wants. Nothing more—children
of America now
disposed, cast out,
recycled and repackaged,
redefined.

III.

We both reach for smoke,
fumbling for a light.
as we turn water
 to philosophy,
pure and beautiful.
 She and I and you,
 faces streaked and wet,
 Jeff Buckley singing,
like a tired addict,
as we kiss goodbye.
Then again, again,
again. Out of breath
and the stench of tears—
wet recollections
drenched in Cruz Campo,
 a toast to *our Spain*,
where we swallowed time,
 beer, weed, and absinth,
and cover our mouths
with each other's hands
holding on to breath,
 holding on to Ka.
a needle between
 us and cobblestone
poking our tired feet
and pushing our arms
around each other.

A woman with flowers—
table to table,
 feeding her children
Euro by Euro.
I buy from habit,
a memory for you.

Glasses clink again,
We drink to roses.

The needle is in
America now
as I reach for more of you,
more stories to tell—

Ginsberg in Lisbon,
playing guitar in the park,
or tears in Lagos.
Chess at my table,
staring at one another
words escaping us.
Black and white photos
of you and I in Tangier,
photos that make us
into memories,
and make others ask questions
about what we have—
the junkie's secrets
left to hide in a poem,
left for you and I.

Section Four: Cities Downstream

The Tree in the Suk
Chefchauan, Morocco

Today,
the bees
in the tree
that shades
the suk don't need
to stray to gardens far away.
Instead, they simply stay and play
in the pollen sticking to the sweet
hyacinth on my window sill that sways
and bows like the vendor on the street
crouching to cover his trinket cart with a dirty sheet
to protect his hundred hands of Fatima from thieves as he prays.
The dull hum
of the bees
competing
with the buzz
from the speaker
anchored atop
the tall tree,
everyone
rooted to
a purpose
of servitude,
to a God,
to a reason
to sit in a quiet
window and think
about the tree covering the suk in a mountain village.

Cicadas

Mecca, Saudi Arabia

Once a year, they come,
wearing into our willow tree,
burrowing anxious larva
into the thick trunk,
singing for sure,
praying perhaps
for strong
children—
constant *yallahs*
swelling and fading
in rhythmic parabolas,
calming the crystal shells
until the day their wings dry.
Then, we return to silence.

A Playground
Shaqlawa, Iraq

The beaten tanks that sit outside the city
do not care about the graffiti
on their treads, the beds of wild basil
growing in their tracks,
or even the children with plastic bowls
on their heads leading the charge
as they straddle the barrels
and throw dirt clods at passing cars
uninterrupted by militia who yawn and smile
as our bus stops just outside the city.

A Reading by Margaret Atwood
Dubai, UAE

The scarf around your neck,
the same shade
as the abaya covering the head
of the woman sitting
next to me on the front row.
As she reaches
to pull the cover
from her face,
exposing long black hair
and a delicately covered bruise,
I feel ashamed,
like a little boy staring
at bare breasts.
Brushing back her hair,
she smiles at me
and doesn't bother
to cover herself again.

At The Wedding Chapel
Baghdad, Iraq

That night, I held
the hand of a child,
his body still
beneath the full
weight of fallen
churchyard walls.
His other hand
beneath the sand
still wrapped around—
I swear to God—
the ring on a smoldered
purple pillow.

We'd found ourselves crawling
through thick smoke, broken
tables and busted water pipes;
bloody, but still breathing,
complaining about tinnitus
and ashes in our mouths
only because to think
of what had really happened
would spoil the calm created
by confusion in the first
short seconds after
the bombs found their crosses.

Two months later,
I sit on my bedroom balcony
drinking a beer—
the same lager
we all shared—
as the night air
carries only the attar
of the trash heaps
down the street,

free from the smell
of smoke and shell.
Still, as I know I always will,
I hold the hand of a child.

A Christmas Scene
Amman, Jordan

There is a Christmas tree
in the entry to the airport,
adorned with flashing lights
and silver tinsel. A girl
in an abaya: she, herself
covered head to toe,
her wrist wrapped
with worry-beads
etched in Arabic script
that catch the camera flash
as she poses for a friend
to take her picture by the tree.

Fig Tree
Duhok, Iraq

1.

In a lush valley between
the Tigris and Euphrates,
a small fig tree bends
toward the morning,
bowing in the understanding
of its own existence.

Across a narrow road, soft enough
to hold the hoof prints of passing
donkeys, I sit in a makeshift
coffee shop—a garage with an open
door and an old pot plugged

2.

Three young girls at the ends
of ropes walk reluctantly,
abayas wet and pressed against
their faces, as their father
at the other end
of the rope pulls harder
with one hand, and waves
a small book in the other.

These girls, tempered
by verse and tradition,
bent backwards by a sterile sickle
still lay in beds next door—
another garage, this one
with a red crescent spray painted
on the door. I feel like such a bastard
for even being here.

3.

I have seen the beauty of a generation dragged, beaten and bruised
through Arab streets at dawn.
The tension of races erased by a common language of law, and God
reduced to an excuse,
reduced to everything
from late homework to cold steel between trembling legs,
reduced in its use to the point of a preposition, or to an amen,
meaningless now, just a period at the end
of a prayer—a big 10-4.

Inshallah—God will see to what will be,
even for a bastard such as me
ashamed of even writing what I see.

Inshallah for my eyes,
Inshallah for a begging boy in London,
Inshallah for Your son in Spain,
Inshallah for an entire city buried in ash,
Inshallah for Easter Sunday,
Inshallah for the rough beast in Cairo, the fists
raised in Syria, Yemen, Lybia, Iran, and Michigan,
Inshallah for the death monuments in Halabja, the
empty prison left the way it was twenty years ago,
Inshallah for Margaret Atwood,
Inshallah for the small child who lies bleeding in my
arms and fell limp as the second scourge of bomb
blasts tried to erase Your existence,
Inshallah to those women in cloth diapers, reduced
to tools because a book, Your book, said so.

4.

As a child in Willow Hill apartments,
I remember sitting on the floor,
listening to my record player
and my grandmother
singing along in the kitchen—
"He loves the birds. He loves the bees.
He even loves a child like me." She is dead now,
and my eyes, though failing, have seen
enough to know this isn't true.

Taking in this view, though,
this green valley, the steep cliffs
cut straight, the wild lilac
stippling the meadow, even the cow
chewing the cud, I know
You are there. That doesn't mean
I have to like You.

Damn You for the joy and for the grief
that makes us fall in prayer on faulted knees.
My knees, now green with grass stains
pressed into the earth beneath
the shadows of leaves on what I want to believe
is the forbidden tree, (the cause of this!),
the fruit that fuels my distaste
for what You have become
and what I believe myself to be.
Give me something, anything—
water from a handful of sand,
or even a plague of darkness to hide
the places we were never meant to see.

Epicenters

1. A Stir of Rough Beasts
        Cairo, Egypt

Fathers carry children into town.
The milk and honey have begun to sour.
The blood of someone's son is on the ground,
as once-quiet hands clench and pound
at guilty guns now hiding in their tower.
Fathers carry children into town.
The circus has arrived and we're the clowns
who let the lion tamer have the power.
The blood of someone's son is on the ground,
his head beneath the hands of men who drown
the sound of coming storms in waves of cowards.
Fathers carry children into town.
Mubarak's clock is finally winding down,
and time has come for all your guns to lower,
now the blood of someone's son is on the ground.
The day to wake rough beasts has come around
and claim from fallen pharaohs what is ours.
Fathers carry children into town.
The blood of someone's son is on the ground.

2. Erbil Libre
    Erbil, Iraq

Stand proud behind your shining sun,
and let your shadows claim your grains
in fields now filled with quiet guns.

The Euphrates carries across the plains,
its bends engorged and pressed to break
beneath the weight of sunken chains.

Forty years of spade and rake
now still above the hard pan drought
allow the weeds to overtake.

They punch the clay in fisted sprouts
and wrap the trunks of olive trees—
too dry, their withered twisted boughs.

They can't sustain the need of leaves
that, brittle, break when winter comes
with winds that spring from Saudi seas.

Stand proud behind your shining sun,
and let your shadows claim your grains
in fields now filled with quiet guns.

With Nawroz comes the mountain flames—
the trail-lit tribal tapestries,
that fear no tears or falling rain.

They blaze and raise the sophistries—
those calls to "keep the monkeys out,"
and "purify the histories."

Drunk on God, they stomp and shout,
"Let all here praise the Father's name,"
while dancing down the river's route.

Once the harvest has been reclaimed
and future yields are finally won,
the gowns can rid their reddened stains.

Stand proud behind your shining sun,
and let your shadows claim your grains
in fields now filled with quiet guns.

3. Nawroz (Revolution Day)
   Hansad Valley, Iraq

Our hands locked in memory
around a dying fire
in a balanced equation—
the zero of the dance
making no man greater,
no woman less than,
the integers erased
among the Arabs, the Kurds.
Even the man who burned
my flag in protest yesterday,
seems to smile at me,
he and I, both lost
in the simple steps—
tapping with our left,
rocking on our right,
our joined hands mocking
the tips of the conflagration
as the ululation
drawn, no, pulled from the throats
of Kurdish women wound
in flowing capes adorned with bangles
silence the crickets' chorus
in the Hansad Valley.

Tomorrow I will go back
to grading students' essays.
The bread maker will roll
his dough and let it rise.
Barzani will shake a finger
at confused cabinet members,
and the soldier will shoulder
his gun for us again:
but now, until this fire dies,
we each amount to nothing.

Pangaea

Tehran, Iran

It hits quick
  and I think
I've had a stroke
  as plaster falls
from wall and ceiling.
  A building crescendo
of bending steel—
  a rhythmic timpani
and swelling squeal
  like hot spoons touched
to dry ice. The skyline,
  gut-punched, doubled over.
Knuckled cross beams
  fisting tenements below
as a silk tie lands
  on a still-standing
clothesline pinned
  with threadbare
farm shirts.

I remember the first time this happened,
sitting close to our new Zenith console
cross-legged and glued to Candlestick Park.
Al Michaels cut mid-sentence
and the steady, almost graceful bow
of the left field flood light leaning
towards the stands, its image intersected
by static lines and interference. Then black.

Then snow. Then gray. Everywhere is gray.
Monochromatic clouds held by no wind
blooming slow from broken windows and a bridge
twisted, pinning a crushed pickup truck,
is all I recall of the last time I sat
and watched the World Series as I steady

now in a door frame,
       legs and arms akimbo
braced between
the flood of then
and the fall of now.

Samaritan Claws
Sharjah, UAE

I would like to believe
the remora clings
to the barnacles beneath
the nurse shark out
of duty, out of the difference
between what we must do
and what we feel compelled
to offer out of understanding—
the legacy of a fortunate traveler
and a chance encounter
with the left-for-dead
remnants of a fellow brother.

But spades and roses,
likened by a simpatico
of similarities exist
for one simple purpose—
the reality of one's true
nature—for the remora
dances in the shallows,
breast to belly,
with it's ravenous victim
simply to survive.

Guard Duty

Muscat, Oman

As I sit outside smoking a cigarette,
a pair of cats patrol the high perimeter fence
casting quick cursory glances at the flakes
of ash trapped in the spears of the spotlights.

One, a Tabby, steps gingerly across the arch
woven in brittle bougainvillea vines
while the other, just an old fat tom,
sets his sights on a moth writhing
in the web of a fortunate widow
who, in turn, patrols her perimeter
as I sit outside smoking a cigarette.

A Sidewalk Café in Damascus

Damascus, Syria

I think I will call the dog
Alfonzo and remember
the beautiful woman
as Aliya simply because I like
these names, and because
she took the time to smile
at a complete stranger
in an ancient city buried
in their phones.

10 o'clock News

Beirut, Lebanon

What I remember of you—
the bomb craters and bullet casings,
faces screaming running past a shaky camera,
men on fire as machines in uniforms stood still
is replaced by a picture on my camera
of an old man standing in a fishing boat
waving at us as he draws
his net across still water.

CPSIA information can be obtained
at www.ICGtesting.com
Printed in the USA
FSOW02n0428250116
16017FS

9 780990 945222